CATASTROPHIC LP

CATASTROPHIC

CATASTROPHIC LP

iUniverse books may be ordered through booksellers or by contacting:

iUniverse
1663 Liberty Drive
Bloomington, IN 47403
www.iuniverse.com
844-349-9409

ISBN: 978-1-6632-1128-6 (sc)
ISBN: 978-1-6632-1129-3 (e)

Print information available on the last page.

iUniverse rev. date: 10/16/2020

Contents

Dear Family 1

Dear Ex 3

Hopeless Romantic 5

Lucienne 7

Sonogram 9

Spanglish 13

Disney 15

Mr. Irrelevant 17

Lost Boy 19

Man's Best Friend 21

Evangeline 23

Guess Who? 25

Giving a Toast 27

Love for My Home 31

Greatest of All Time 35

Poet tree with a loose leaf 37

Warning: Suicide Watch 39

Dear Family

Lately I've been thinking about what you do for me
I know I don't thank you for everything
But I am thankful for the help and support
And I know there's more
Of a good child in me
That we haven't seen
With school and the stress
My emotions have gotten the best
Of me
And the
Adrenaline
From you guys yellin'
Eventually
Get to me
And puts me lower than I've ever been
Our anger turns into venom
I said all that so maybe we can fix
Our emotions so they don't get mixed
Anyway I love you all
And I hope you never fall
The way I did. Keep up the good work
And when you stumble rub off the dirt
Sorry if I ever hurt you with my words

Sincerely,
Andrew

Dear Ex

Ever since we split I've been a mess
I miss having your head on my chest
You made me feel whole
Even when we were outside I felt like I was home
I never wanted you to leave me alone
It still hurts that we had to let go
Of each other
It feels like I got hit by a band made of rubber
Anyway, how's your mother?
Believe it or not I think about her too
In our relationship she was the glue
She helped to keep us close
She's a sweet person and deserves a toast
For the person that she is
To continue,
I sort of miss you
I've been writing poems in memory
Of what we use to be
So much bliss and tranquility
We use to be king and queen
Now apparently you don't know me
It's so funny how I went from honey
To nobody
I didn't have a whole lot of money
But I had lots of time to spend
I'm blessed I spent it with you
There was nothing else I'd rather do
I loved going to the movies
We'd see anything and I'd be happy

All because you were with me
Giving me kissies
And putting bliss within me
We're so close but yet so far
They say X spots the mark
Now there's a dark
Spot in my heart
Where you used to take part
Now it hurts to start
They day I want to decay but it's not smart
To just lie and fall apart
I guess I should've known you'd ditch me from the start
I still loved you even with a broken heart
I adored you like there was no tomorrow
I'm not saying this to degrade your sorrow
Since I still care for you like King Kong did for Ann Darrow
You know if you fell I'd follow
I hope you take care and be there
For your daughter Blair
And for your husband too
Hopefully the love he gives you is brand-new
And nothing suspicious
I had an opportunity and I wasn't going to miss this
I needed to tell you how I felt
Before I continued to melt

Sincerely,
Whatever you want to call me

Hopeless Romantic

Day in and day out
I think about
What's going to occur
I can't see through the blur
But I believe good will come
No matter where it's from
I pray for love
Not sure if he heard above
But I'm still waiting for life
To guide me to my wife
I've been so lost for a while
So I'm in denial
That my prayers were answered
Heart feeling shattered
All this time alone makes me think
That I'm only floating just to sink
Maybe I need to wear a mask
Or hide everything from my past
These ideas are bad
They won't make the relationship last
Wanting to hug and cuddle
But I'm in the struggle
Of finding someone good for me
Do I stay here or head out to sea?
I'm not one of those wack boys
I see my love as a person not a toy
Those kids want all girls to give them attention
I want one girl to give me all of her affection
But no one is looking my way

My heart decays
I'm trying all healing methods
But the pain grows every second
Doesn't matter what I choose to do
I have to solve this mystery like Scooby-Doo
I hope to do no wrongs
I want to keep her happy forever long
I'll make sure her heart stays whole
Because I know what it's like to feel alone
And scared I will always be there I'll do the best that I can
For her as a person and as her man
She won't be treated as luxury
If it's hard
To keep us apart
It must be easy
To come together completely
I'm tired of seeing the girl of my dreams
I want to see the girl of my life
Am I asking for too much? Am I in too much of a rush?
I don't want to hush or seem like I'm causing a fuss
But I'm going psycho and losing control like Russ

Lucienne

They ask me to write about what I'm lovin'
I instantly think of my little cousin
Who I love three thousand times a dozen
I've only seen her once and
I adore her little hands
I hope to see her before she gets a man
She's growing so fast. When I see her I'll latch on like a cast
I wish to make her laugh so when she looks back at the past
She remembers the bad times last
I see her pretty face and tears fill my eyes because in time
I want one of mine
I dream to be a father to a daughter so I can walk on water
I can't wait much longer
If you dare to hurt her you'll get slaughtered
They are and will be blessings
With all this love my heart is compressing
I love them both equally
Even when I can't be there physically
I'll be with you spiritually

Sonogram

I wait and wait for the date that's saved
To welcome my baby Avalon-Grace
Or should I pick a different name?
I adore Abigail-Ophelia but they say the name is lame
But it's my child
It's better than something wild
Like table or bed sheet
Or even horse stable and rebel fleet
These thoughts of having a child make me loose balance
I know raising a child is a challenge
I won't lie to them like I'm under oath
I'd be there to help with the growth
Both physically and mentally
My whole life is in one picture
I can't wait to kiss her
And hold her in the little swaddle
I have to be the best role model
For my little miracle
My chemical of love is spiritual
Plus it's visible
She not just an individual
She's a reason to live
And to forget the pain within
Higher power forgive my sins
So I can be free
With the little me
I want to be the best me I can be
For my baby
Tell her "I love you" on the daily

Say she's beautiful till I drive her crazy
Even then I'd still say it, well maybe
I don't to upset my little lady
What if she likes star wars?
It'll be my fault of course
I'm just obsessing with this life
I want to live it every day and night
These are my hopes and dreams
But peeps tell me to chill because I'm 19
Ah crickets, jiminy please help me
The way you did with the wooden boy
Tell the people my love isn't a decoy. I really want to share joy
With my baby and my lady
I think about this on the daily
"Why does this need to be said aloud?"
I want my dreams to be heard with ultra sound
I want my wonderful daughter
Who comes from her beautiful mother
I can't promise a perfect father but I'll tend to her at night
When I hear her cry
For an aid because that's the life I made
Ain't nothing getting in the way
Of me
And my baby
I'll keep the smile on her pretty face
I'll keep the food on her dinner plate
Keep clothes on her back
Keep the roof above in tact
Hold her in my arms as long as I can
Before she ends up in arms of another man
I pray that the higher power has a plan
To help her grow
And to help her know
That she has more than a dad

She has a father who's glad
To the core
That she was his daughter and more
She was the glue to his broken heart
And the reason why it didn't continue to fall apart
With that laugh and smile
It could light up the world for miles
Hopefully the mom stays with them
So she can help with the teachings of wisdom
Help protect against the viruses like an immune system
I'd love my family like no tomorrow
In my heart is where I'd keep the photos
I've got names for my future mamas
I can't wait to hear the words, "I love you papa"

Spanglish

People use to tease me because I don't follow
Stereo types y no yo habo espanol
Mucho or ever
I'm Mexican no matter the weather
It's what I am, not what I do or what I say
So pinche puta madre get out of my way
Esto es lo que voy a hacer
Porque quiero vivir la vida que quiero tener
No la vida que quieres para mi
En ingles, I'm going to be me for me
Not for you
You act a fool
Let me understand another thing
Why do I have to be speaking Spanish or eating rice and beans?
I like Applebee's too but you're just rude though
Yo veo Disney no telemundo
No we don't all illegally cross the boarder
Okay trump supporter?
Trying to deport us for speaking espanol
Ya'll gotta go
Back to your casas
I'll be in mine making masa
Para mi comida
While listening to Selena's
Not Gomez, Quintanilla
No more dissing
Just reminiscing
About our pasts
We all want love to outlast the bad

There are bad people but don't compare them to the rest
Voy decir otra vez
Esto es lo que voy a hacer
Porque quiero vivir la vida que quiero tener
No la vida que quieres para mi
En ingles, I'm going to be me for me
Not for you
Because you act a fool

Disney

I've loved the mouse since I was a boy
I had him as a stuffed toy
Let me tell you a story
We loved the parks sunny or pouring
We would act goofy
We'd feel like we were in the movies
We went to never land
And wonderland
We even had an adventure
With a toad and found treasure
With pirates
We saw a sith lord and got quiet
I was munching on popcorn
Then someone said they were mad at a horn
Anyway
I was too afraid
To go on the thundery mountain
Everyone always shouted
Or did that come from the scary home?
If you dared to go in there you were on your own
Luckily there was a honey bear
With friends who liked to share
Stories and sing songs
My favorite wasn't too long
It was about a jungle. They had it in a hard cover
And there was another about a fish who lost his mother
It's hard to find
I wish I could rewind time
So I can be happy

Like the time I was able to see
Roger Rabbit
I couldn't believe it happened
I also remember staying at the end of each day
We'd stay to watch the parade
We went so much I bet they remembered our names
Oh it was incredible
Smiling was inevitable
I love their work from Steamboat Willy
To the wooden boy and the brotherly grizzlies
There's also Coco, Good Dinosaur, Inside Out, and Cars
Because that's just what my picks are
It's sad we can't go back due to prices
I used to love thinking I had my license,
Soaring with elephants,
And even playing with insects
Was a blast and I couldn't go to bed
As the founder once said,
"To all who come to this happy place, Welcome"

Mr. Irrelevant
(The Last Pick)

I was never the top gun or the top Hun
I was just there so someone could make fun
Of me on how I was so ugly
No girl would hug me
Growing up I was never approached
They looked at me as if I was a roach
And treated me like a horse on a stage coach
But apparently they want to go with a guy
Who won't wipe a tear from their eye
He's self-centered
Yet he appears to be better
Than me
A "man" with lovely
Attributes
They practically chose to be abused
Not necessarily physically but emotionally
I'd show them how love is supposed to be
I'd have them at my side, never alone
I can't just leave them on their own
I can't just stay out of the way
The other guys would control her like a video game
I'm not like the special "men"
I did have a confused past but that is
what I outlast, I've made amends
I give compliments
From the heart
They say it to spread your legs apart
I'm not a monster for your cookie

Says who? Says me
That type of person is something I'll never be
I love bliss and tranquility
Say goodbye to being neglected
With me you'll get respected
I was never pretty so I got rejected
The majority of those women were shallow
So I was left hanging like the gallows
I never really got it
Then one day I thought it
Was because I was a bad person
Or I just wasn't what they were searchin'
For
My heart was blown up with C4
Now I'm walking around trying to find
The pieces thinking they're side by side
But nothing in life is in a line
Sometimes not even your state of mind
To move on, well that's hard
I'm attempting to staple my broken heart
And make it stronger than ever
I'm getting rid of the rope that's around my neck
Since I'm not like the rest
I don't care about thighs and breast
I'm a good guy with romantic intentions
I just have a rusted engine
And please pay attention
I'm not going to cheat
I want to sweep you off your feet
And carry you into the sunset
To lay you in bed to rest
I'd wrap you like some foil
And treat you but not let you go spoiled

Lost Boy

Growing up I had a map that guided me to never land
That's why it took long to become a man
Now that I am, I do what I can
Like building a damn
But it doesn't stop the flow
Of my rows you know
I got the vibe of the west coast
I don't get bread but I receive toasts
I'm getting far but I don't do the most
My life is a show and I'm not even the host
That praised ghost
Is what sunk my boat
Now I have to find another way to stay afloat
If I was still in never land
I could've asked Peter Pan
To help me through the sea
With the dust of pixie
I'm getting air lifted
Today is an ad; I knew I should've skipped it
Life comes in all sorts of shapes but mine is a circle
I'm so tired I'm turning purple
I get pushed away like Urkel
I'm confused; I can't find the words to stay on track
Stability is what I lack
I've lost weight but I want my patience back
Because I loved helping people
Keeping everything nice and peaceful
Now I have to try and survive in the dark
I'm a soldier who's at war with his heart

My weapon is my mind
I can't find the ability to design a new line and
I have to write the same rhymes twice
The words are taking a beating
And they're losing meaning
I need to do some spring cleaning
Like maybe I'm not falling, I'm just leaning
I'm not nowhere, I'm in a place I've never been
I don't live for the moment. I make a moment to live in
I don't just want to survive
I want to feel alive
I don't walk a lonely road,
I walk the road alone
I live to dream
But die in my nightmares in my sleep
I want the pain to go away
So I don't live with the errors of yesterday,
And I can live for what I can be tomorrow
No more sorrow
I attempt to ball like Kobe
But I'm still slowly decomposing
I have bulbs that aren't glowing
I have or's so I keep rowing
Forward
Even when my self-esteem is lowered
I'm so mental
I speak with a pencil
I'm still a car even if I'm a rental
I'm hurt yet still sentimental
I had to write this before I got arthritis
For better days I'll stay praying like a mantis
It's hard being stranded especially when
life isn't the way you planned it

Man's Best Friend

When I was a little kid
I wanted a dog to play with
Then one day this little guy came into my life
My joy was flying high like a kite
I will never forget the years of fun we had
You made me so glad
All the road trips and times we played in the yard
I'd squeak your toy then you'd unravel like yarn
We did so much in so little time
I like dogs and I love that you were mine
You were my light in the fog
You were my little brother but obviously a dog
That didn't change the way I loved and cared for you
Playing is all I wanted to do with you
I am blessed to have been able to see you after school
From kindergarten to high school
And then some
I miss you a ton
It's hard coming home to know I won't be seeing you
I don't know what I'm supposed to do
The time was so pleasant
I still hear and feel your presence
You were such a blessing, have fun in doggy heaven

P.s. Say hi to grandpa for me

Evangeline

When I see her, I get to huggin'
I adore my little munchkin
I love watching her grow and I hope she knows
I'm going to be there through rain or snow
She keeps the glow in my heart so I don't fall apart
She makes light out of the dark
I love and adore her like no tomorrow
Any moment with her contains no sorrow
Always laughing and having fun
Including her going on a run
When she sees me since she thinks
I'm going to chase her. She's my shrink
And the link that holds me together
Through my blizzard and stormy weather
I'm the word and she's the letters
I'm a good person, she makes me better
Evangeline I love you
And I adore you too

Love,
Cousin Andrew

Guess Who?

When I was fresh
I thought about this girl over the rest
To me she was the best
I still have that pain in my chest
Because I'm a wreck and a mess
Since she went on stage with caution I thought she was adorable
This kind of beauty is unaffordable
But apparently she had the money
To be so lovely
Any guy would be lucky
To have her as their significant other
Any child would be blessed to have her as their mother
Just look at her smile
That could make you happy for a while
Even when she's upset
She does her best
To set aside the hate you give
That won't dictate how she lives
Even when she was a little girl
She was already taking on the world
I don't get how
I turned a "wow"
Into a "I want you"
This is a mystery like Scooby-doo
I guess the desire increased
Since I can't even walk on my feet
My mind is playing tricks on me
This odd obsession helped me get
through some of my depression

This is just a short history for the long road
Without you I would have never gone into beast mode
Or even found a motive
I adore you and you already know this
Because of you
I had something to pursue
I wanted a musical life and I thought about being an actor
These were ideas and you were the deciding factor
If she ever fell I wanted to catch her
I could never blame her for trying
She's probably thinking "why me?"
I can sense her good heart and she truly did inspire me
When I was feeling low, your smile brought me to a higher key
Sorry this was brought up all suddenly
I can't keep this inside for all of eternity

Giving a Toast

These ladies are like Amy Adams
Their beauty is hard to fathom
For starters I was four years old
I didn't know love but love knew me
so I was able to grow a rose
For Rhianna
Because apparently I viewed her as my baby mama
But I didn't want to cause drama
With Fergie
Then again I wanted Sonny to give me
A chance
I thought of her and started to dance
In my head I felt like these crushes couldn't last
For long
And of course I was wrong
I still view them as pretty
I guess their beauty is something I'll always see
Because it stays with me like beauty on Cara Delevingne
Also I don't have to go
On 50 first dates to know
That Drew Barrymore
Is adorable; haven't you seen E.T. before?
The blondie from four Christmases is cute too
She eats Reese's with a spoon
I guess that's pretty awesome
Sorry my words are a little off I'm just awestruck
My breath has been taken
Like the time when the force was awakened

There's a spell over me that was casted by Emma
Watson and all I can say is "oh man"
Like the way I did when I first saw Lindsey Lohan
I know I won't meet them today but maybe in Tomorrowland
To move forward you have to have grit like Britt Robertson
She'd be a good friend like Jennifer Aniston
And Allison
Miller
I want to imply I admire a lady officer
Externally and internally they are so gorgeous
Like Haley Upton and Kim Burgess
They always seem to leave me wordless
And my diaphragm contracts
That's why I can't react
In the situations they have me in
I'm trying to live a sweet life like Barbra Palvin
I'm not a good fisher but I can still carry a princess
I'll pay Dejong one a visit
And write her freedom like Hilary Swank
All these ladies are too pretty to rank
They're all queens like Padme
Award them tiaras
And don't forget to mention Kate Mara
Even Hunter, Joey, Billie, and Brie
Especially the three carpenters from the valley
I know I wasn't always a gentleman
But I wanted to give compliments and recognition as settlement
To the ones that inspire me, like Serena
Williams and Charity Witt
They've got great ambition and grit
I'll show my daughter a pic
Of all of you
And tell her she can be like you
Because there's nothing in this world you can't do

I know I mainly spoke on looks
But I dearly admire the inspiration you cook
If I didn't say your name or give you a reference
You're all still full of beauty and power;
trust me it's truly splendid

Love for My Home

If this city could walk, it'd go anywhere it puts its mind to
If this city could talk it'd say, "I'm nothing without you"
If this city had emotion
It would be broken
Not due to the riots
Or the loss of Bryant
But due to the fight
Through the day and night
That makes us question our life's position
It won't be solved by signing a petition
We don't need permission to keep wishin'
We are the ammunition for the ambition
to complete this mission
Community is majority communication and all of unity
Together we live happily
Bliss and tranquility
Do this not only for your family
But for the city
Be the spark that lights the fire
For the burning desire
To make this a better place
For us to welcome a new face
Each and everyday
Be the change that lights the way
Don't let hope decay
There's too much to throw away
Let's throw a party or a ball
We need all of ya'll
In order to celebrate

The abolishment of hate
There's no reason to have complicated
Life caused by other beings
Let's just dance and sing
I know I haven't necessarily done things clearly or respectfully
And I'm not forcing you to follow me
Because at the end of the day you water the seeds
You planted
We all have our parts in making a beautiful planet
One thing I wanted to say is that you're not better than me
Okay your parents make lots of money and can afford a balcony
That doesn't mean you have the right to talk down on me
In sports some of the goats don't even gloat
You're a yacht, I'm a lil boat
We're both on the same water and we're both afloat
My words aren't for show
I want to let you know
Through cold or stormy weather
We're better together
No more silence
No more violence
Together we end the purple and turn green like the trees
That Mother Nature gave us to breathe
I want to lead but there's no need to vote for me
I voice and act but I don't do it heroically
We all need oxygen
Our sisters and brother are not boxing gyms
Wipe their tears and hold 'em
Poppa is doing laundry, help him fold em
Momma is making bread, help her roll em
It's okay to switch roles
So we no longer carry the toll
Of the past like a cast
On our hearts or mine

Because in the end of time
We'll all be fine
No more begging for dimes
Or copper
No more begging for food like hopper
The planet is dirty and we're the soap
Let's rise up; we're earth's last hope

Greatest of All Time

You took care of us when we were kids
You loved us even when we threw fits
You taught us to fill our hearts bliss
Your wisdom is something I'll truly miss
The way you spoke kept us woke
How much you loved us is something I'll never know
The value of your love is too high for us to count
I wish I could tell you that I loved you with the same amount
I'm sorry that those words never really came out of my mouth
I'm sorry for the times when I caused conflict
I was just a kid
I wish I could get rid
Of my mistakes
That made you have a bad day.
Through all the rain you loved me anyway
I loved our trips to breakfast
Those moments of bliss with you I will truly miss
At the end of the day you are away
From the pain that made your skies grey
You are at rest with your love
Please watch over us
From above
It's been hard knowing you're not here
I want to say I love you to your ear
Instead of sending the words spiritually
You were always the better part of me
Now I'll never be the same
You taught me the game
Of baseball and much more

I hate going to your house and not having you open the door
For us when we get there
This pain I can't even bear
The love you gave us was rare like winning a prize at the fair
I try to knock on god's door and no one is there
I want to see you again
So I can put the pain to an end
Of me not being able to say goodbye
In my eye
You were the twinkle
My heart continues to wrinkle
Most of all, when I start reminisce
I realize that you would never miss
The opportunity
To say you loved me
I decided to write a poem
Because it's the best way I show emotion
You're a legend like David Freese
Great Grandpa, Rest in Peace

Poet tree with a loose leaf

I think my issue is feeling loved
I feel like there is a higher power above
Guiding me on where the light could be
But here's the thing, I can't believe in something I've never seen
How many times do I have to be on my knees?
And say, "lord forgive me please
So I can live freely I'm so sorry
For tripping as if I'm on Bacardi"
I want to live and party
But all I see is black and white like Marty
All beautiful elements faded
Through this pain that's been created
Now I feel caged in and deranged
The pain stays the same every day no matter which way I sway
I have to protect my name in this game
In order to obtain and sustain the strength of my membrane
And I can go away from being insane
There are times where I'm okay then I go "bang"
Like a tank that contains propane
Anyway, I was going to say
I need a friend to help prevent my brain
From going down the drain
And help pass the cloud so it won't rain
I have one now but she is going to switch lanes
I knew eventually I'd have to change
Mentally because potentially
I could meet the one I'm meant to be
With for a long while
I've traveled the Nile and my emotions are in a pile

Now they're becoming unraveled but lost in gravel
I have to battle my cattle in order to sit upon a saddle
I don't want to be a snake but my heart is
rattled and has become fragile
This is so wack, my heart is black
And I can't sit back and relax while I'm
flat on my back like a mat
I'm carrying weight like a rack
I want my pack to acknowledge this fact
But it'll probably lead to a nuclear reaction
Since I'm already broken into a fraction
I want love, no more cracking apart my heart
And treating me as if I'm from mars
I'm not an extra terrestrial
I know I'm special
Since I'm a basket case
The tears on my casket would've filled the vase
To the flowers that would be sour and stale
Had I gone pale when I tried to bail
My freshman year
Now I fight tears when I look in the mirror
because all that appears is a boy in fear
That no one wants him near
I train hard to get far and I write bars to erase scars
I'm not who I used to be, can you tell us apart??

Warning: Suicide Watch
(Not just for me)

I ask for a reason to stay
And everyday
I find one
But within the next hours, I have none
None, as in no why to be alive
Now I have to find light through my blind eyes
That explains why I'm not in a straight line
Swerving and curving
While I'm learning the road
I don't know here I'm going to go
I hope to not end up like Mr. Toad
Dead on the side of the road
Hey look there's a rope
So does that mean there's hope?
Or am I too much of a dope that's traveling a downward slope
Hopping around like an antelope while trying to cope
The pain like my eyes contain soap
I'm born on Valentine's Day yet I'm not cupid
Maybe I'm just stupid
There's no Ricola to heal this corona
It won't even decrease the chances of Ebola
It doesn't want me to be
Able to see a better me
It's trying to take my head like a guillotine
This agony leaves me
Trapped as if I'm in a chamber full of nova six
Am I falling for tricks?
Damn it

I'm a silly rabbit
Going on to the next cut like a barber
My mind gets attacked like Pearl Harbor
Crazy thoughts stay open 24/7
When I close my eyes am I going to heaven?
Or will I fight through tomorrow
And see smiles while I'm in sorrow
Do you guys have joy I can barrow
So I can heal from a heart rupture?
I need nice medication, no acupuncture
No pretty girl wants me to hug her
And I want to have a baby mother
If you listen to me
It's a wish and a dream
I pray for its happening
This is my motive
And some can't seem to notice
Anything past me being nineteen
I don't take your shit lightly
I don't know if it's just me
But it might possibly be that I seem to be
Evil because the words I use should be illegal
But I do care for people
I don't want a sequel with this pain that's so lethal
Maybe one day I'll go to hell when I sleep
Because when I wake I'll be living the dream
With my wife and kid
Smile ear to ear and say this is it
I made it to the summit
I never had to submit
To the agony
That had me
Thinking about taking my own
I'm tempted to pick up the phone

And call the number to tell them my wrists
Are slit
The continue to drip on the floor
Forget that. They're beginning to pour
Now I feel more alive than I did before
Yet I feel empty like a store
During a pandemic
This is all truth. If I never meant it
I would've never said it
I would have kept it embedded
In my head so when I go to bed
I wake up brain dead
All of these parasites that paralyze my sights
Sadly there's closed ears and open mouths
They hate when we shed tears and pout
But they continue to shut us down
Saying it's a choice to frown
They don't know what it's like to go around town
Being pushed away like Erkel
Now my heart is purple
Since I'm at war with it and it fell apart
I even have battle wounds and I've had PTSD from the start
I hate living in the dark, even during the day it's hard
To play cards since the hearts
Should be red
But as I said
Before, my blood has poured on the floor
Now I'm just décor for
A new horror movie
I'm blended like a smoothie
None of my words have been soothing
Neither is life but I keep moving
I'm going to be me
But suicidal thoughts leave me

Haunted
I'm tired of not being wanted
Am I going insane? Well maybe
If so, can you save me?
Imagine you going through this daily
It'd drive you crazy

Printed in the United States
By Bookmasters